Local Ecology

Kay Davies
and
Wendy Oldfield

Wayland

Starting Science

Books in the series

Animals
Day and Night
Electricity and Magnetism
Floating and Sinking
Food
Hot and Cold
Information Technology
Light
Local Ecology
Materials
Plants
Pushing and Pulling
Rocks and Soil
The Senses
Skeletons and Movement
Sound and Music
Time and Change
Waste
Water
Weather

About this book

Local Ecology looks at the interactions between living things. Children are encouraged to investigate different habitats and discover for themselves why plants and animals live in their own special places. They learn that factors like pollution, people, and the position of sites reflect the type of plants and animals that will colonize areas. They learn how human influences can change habitats and be detrimental to plant and animal life.

This book provides an introduction to methods in scientific enquiry and recording. The activities and investigations are designed to be straightforward but fun, and flexible according to the abilities of the children. The main picture and its commentary may be taken as an introduction to the topic or as a focal point for further discussion. Each chapter can form a basis for extended topic work.

Teachers will find that in using this book, they are reinforcing the other core subjects of language and mathematics. Through its topic approach ***Local Ecology*** covers aspects of the original National Science Curriculum for key stage 1 (levels 1 to 3), for the following Attainment Targets: Exploration of science (AT 1), The variety of life (AT 2), Processes of life (AT 3), Human influences on the Earth (AT 5) and Earth and atmosphere (AT 9) as well as for the amended Curriculum: Scientific investigation (AT 1) and Life and living processes (AT 2).

First published in 1992 by
Wayland (Publishers) Ltd
61 Western Road, Hove
East Sussex BN3 1JD, England

Typeset by Kalligraphic Design Ltd, Surrey
Printed in Italy by
Rotolito Lombarda S.p.A., Milan
Bound in Belgium by Casterman S.A.

British Library Cataloguing in Publication Data
Davies, Kay 1946
1. Local ecology – (Starting science)
I. Title II. Oldfield, Wendy
III. Archer, Rebecca IV. Series
574.5

ISBN 0 7502 0288 2

Editor: Cally Chambers

CONTENTS

All the words that first appear in **bold** in the text are explained in the glossary.

HOME BASE

Have you ever found a spider in your bath? They live in the cracks and **crevices** in your home. They eat flies which come indoors to find scraps of your food.

Our homes and gardens can be **habitats** for many living things.

A habitat is a place where certain animals and plants live.

Look for creatures or plants that share your home or garden with you.

Look under rugs, in corners and on window frames.

Look outside for any plants growing on bricks or in cracks.

Keep a daily diary of the living things you find. Can you find any of them every day?

Nobody has lived in this house for many years. It has become a wild habitat for lots of plants and animals.

Gardens can be full of colourful flowers. We can choose the plants we want and look after them carefully.

GARDEN CENTRE

All sorts of plants and animals like the places we prepare for our flowers.

Gardens, window-boxes or tubs can attract many visitors.

In summer, fill a tub with garden soil and put plants in it. Leave it outside. Make sure you water it every day.

Does anything else grow in your pot?
Does it have any visitors such as butterflies or ladybirds?
Draw your pot to show the living things you find.

Look at people's gardens. You will find that plants and animals enjoy gardens as much as we do.

There are lots of vegetables growing in the garden.
The gardener is **harvesting** potatoes to be eaten.

WHAT A PEST!

Some of the visitors we have in our gardens and farms are not welcome.
Pests suck the goodness from plants.
Weeds spoil our food plants. They block off light from the sun and take goodness from the soil.

Pesticides kill weeds and pests but they can also spoil the soil for useful creatures. We can use less harmful substances.

Mix some soap and water in a spray can. Spray the pests you find on bean plants or roses.

Come back the next day to see if you have got rid of the harmful pests.

STREET LIFE

Cracks in pavements and roadsides collect soil. It is blown in by the wind. It is left by people's shoes.

Tiny creatures build their homes in the cracks. Plants grow there too.

Choose two paving stones outside your school. Look at them for signs of plants and animals every day.

Lay white paper over your paving stones and rub hard with a crayon.

Draw some pictures of the living things you have found and label them.

Stick them on your rubbings of the paving stones. Add another picture when you see something new.

The children are on their way to school.
There is a whole world of life underneath their feet.

FRESH AIR

Dirty air is bad for living things. It is spoiled and **polluted**. It can kill plants and make animals ill.

Collect leaves from trees in different places in your town. Keep a note of where they come from.

Dip each leaf into a different bowl of clean water. Use a paintbrush to wipe all the dirt off into the water.

Pour the water through a paper napkin in a funnel.

Which is the dirtiest place in your town?

When the paper napkins have dried, stick them on a poster. Label which part of town the dirt came from.

The roads are very busy. **Car exhausts** fill the air with dirt, dust and **fumes**.

The woodpecker has pecked a hole in the tree for its nest. It finds insects to eat in the bark of the tree.

TREE HOUSE

A tree can be a home, shelter and food store.

Squirrels spend most of their time in trees. They build a **drey** for their babies there, eat the nuts and keep safe from animals that would like to eat them.

Find a group of trees. Watch for creatures that visit them. Do any birds live there?

Choose one tree with low branches to investigate.

Search the bark and leaves for insects.

Lay a sheet on the ground under the tree. Gently shake a branch. If you need help, ask an adult. What falls on to your sheet?

HEDGEROW

Our hedges make perfect homes for all kinds of creatures. They are good hiding places and safe shelters from the wind and rain.

Mammals, birds and insects make their homes there. Some like to live among the roots underground. Others live in the dark under the leaves.
Spiders set their traps where they can find a meal.

Look for creatures in garden or farm hedgerows.
Can you match the numbers to the creatures in this picture?

Hedgerows mark out the fields and stop farm animals wandering away. They make good wildlife habitats too.

The fallen leaves lie on the forest floor. The **leaf litter** will be broken down to become part of the soil.

GONE TO EARTH

The soil is alive! It is full of plants and animals.

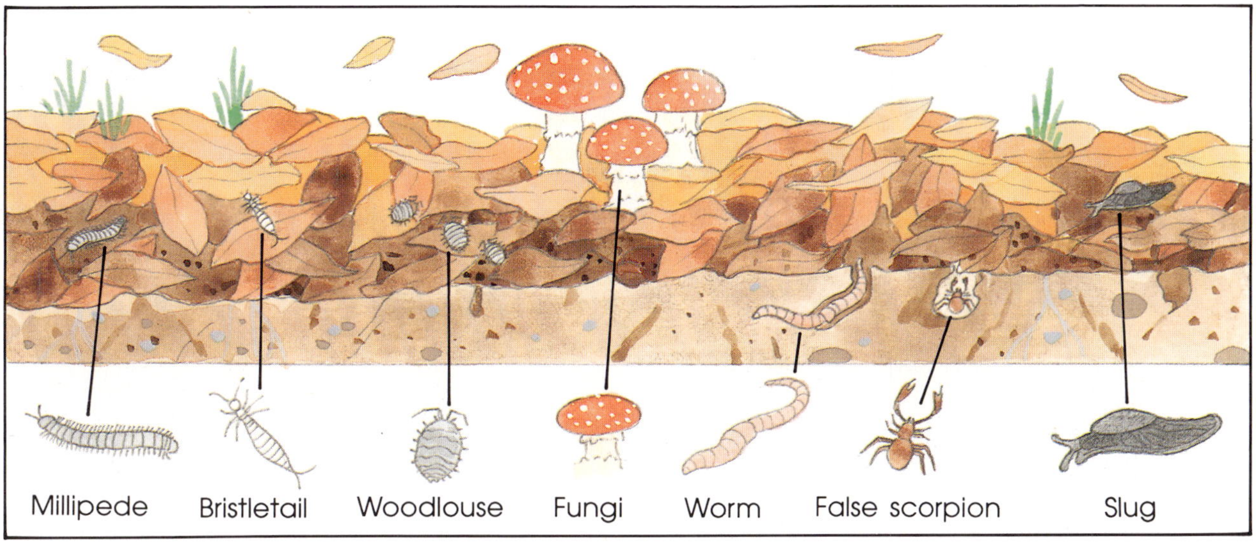

The creatures that live in the forest soil find lots of food. They eat other animals, fallen leaves and roots of plants.

Fill a deep plastic tank with soil and leaf litter from a forest or wood.

Cover it with a dark cloth.

Water the soil every day.

Lift the cloth to see what creatures are living inside your tank.

The railway is no longer used. It has become wild and overgrown. Many plants and animals live there now.

WILD THINGS

Wasteland is a good place for grasses and wild flowers to grow.

Their seeds are already in the soil, or are carried there by the wind or on animals' fur and feet.

If they are left alone, grasses and other plants make flowers and seeds.

Insects drink **nectar** from the flowers. Mice and birds eat the seeds.

Look at some waste ground to see what you can find.
Plant some grass seeds in a pot or tray. Water them every day. Watch the grass grow through the summer.
Grass flowers are tiny. Use a **magnifying glass** to look at them. Does your grass grow seeds?

CRACKS AND CREVICES

Some walls are dry on one side and **damp** on the other. The dry side faces the sun. When it rains the shady side often stays damp.

Find a wall to investigate.

Which plants and animals can you find on the dry side?

Are they different to those on the shady side?

Collect thick blocks of polystyrene.

Stick them together to build a wall.

Draw and cut out pictures of the plants and creatures you have found.

Stick them on the correct side of the wall.

The old wall is full of cracks and crevices. There are places for plants to grow and animals to hide.

COOL POOL

You can make your own pond habitat in an **aquarium**.

Put some gravel in an aquarium.

Half fill it with water from a local pond.

Add some leaf litter from the bottom of the pond.

Collect plants and animals from the pond.

Use large stones to fix plants to the bottom.

Find duckweed to float on the top.

Water snails will live happily in your aquarium. You may see the **larvae** of insects in the pond water.

How many of these creatures can you find in a pond habitat?

Don't cover your tank. Air mixes with the water and keeps it fresh. The air keeps the pond alive.

Plants, fish and tiny creatures all live in the pond. Everything they need is in the water or air around it.

It's fun to spend a day at the seaside. If we leave anything behind, it becomes pollution on the beach.

BUCKET AND SPADE

Some things belong on the seashore. These are natural things, such as sand, rocks and pebbles. There may also be living plants, animals or their remains washed up by the sea.
Some things do not belong in the sea or on the shore.
Tin cans and plastic bottles are rubbish left behind by people. They cause pollution.

If you can, search along a beach.
On a circle of sand-coloured card draw pictures of all the objects you find. Pin a circle of sea-blue card on top, with a section cut out.

Turn the waves to see what is washed up on your beach.

FUN AND GAMES

Visit your local park. Watch to see how people use the park, and what plants and animals live there.

Can you find any of these habitats in your park?

Make a list of the habitats. Keep a record of what people are doing there and the living things you see.

Make a large map of your park. Draw pictures to stick on it to show what lives there and how people use it.

GLOSSARY

Aquarium A see-through tank made for keeping water creatures and plants.
Car exhausts The unpleasant and sometimes harmful waste gases that cars make.
Crevices Deep cracks between rocks and stones.
Damp Slightly wet.
Drey A nest made of twigs and leaves in which squirrels rest and have their babies.
Fumes Unpleasant or harmful gases.
Habitat A place where certain plants and animals live together.
Harvesting Collecting food to be eaten.
Larvae Young insects at the stage in their lives between being eggs and adults.
Leaf litter Pieces of dead and rotting leaves.
Magnifying glass A specially curved piece of glass that makes objects look bigger.
Mammals Animals whose babies feed on their mothers' milk.
Nectar The sweet juice of a flower that insects and some birds drink.
Pesticides Substances used to kill harmful insects and weeds.
Polluted When the surroundings we live in are spoiled by substances that are added to them.
Wasteland Land which people no longer use.

FINDING OUT MORE

Books to read:

A to Z Animals by Beverley Mathias & Ruth Thomson (Franklin Watts, 1989)
All About Baby Animals by Michael Chinery (Kingfisher, 1989)
Animals by Kay Davies and Wendy Oldfield (Wayland, 1990)
My Class Looks After Pets by Vicky Lee (Franklin Watts, 1986)
My Feather by Jane Mainwaring (A & C Black, 1989)
Plants by Kay Davies and Wendy Oldfield (Wayland, 1991)
Waste by Kay Davies & Wendy Oldfield (Wayland, 1990)
Water by Kay Davies and Wendy Oldfield (Wayland, 1991)

Series that include useful books:

Baby Animals (Franklin Watts)
First Nature Books by Gunilla Ingves (A & C Black)
First Pets (Franklin Watts)
Keeping Minibeasts (Franklin Watts)
Life Cycles (Wayland)
Look at Animals (Franklin Watts)
Nature Study (Wayland)
Through the Seasons (Wayland)
Use Your Eyes (Wayland)

PICTURE ACKNOWLEDGEMENTS

Ecoscene 20; Eye Ubiquitous 23; Chris Fairclough 11; PHOTRI 14; Tony Stone Worldwide 6, 8, 13, 15 top, 17, 18, 25, 26, 27 top; Wayland Picture Library (Zul Mukhida) *cover*, 9, 10 both, 12 both, 15 bottom, 19, 21, 22, 27 bottom, 29; ZEFA 5, 7.
Artwork illustrations by Rebecca Archer.
The publishers would also like to thank the parents and children for their kind co-operation in making this book.

INDEX

Page numbers in **bold** indicate subjects shown in pictures, but not mentioned in the text on those pages.